Pursuing Project Excellence

Six Ideas to Improve Your Projects

Bob Jewell, PMP

Pursuing Project Excellence

Six Ideas to Improve Your Projects

First edition published 2016.

ISBN: 978-0-9860894-0-4
ISBN: 978-0-9860894-1-1 (e-book)

Library of Congress Control Number:

Credits
Copy Editor   Kathleen Green, Positively Proofed, Plano, TX
                                                info@PositivelyProofed.com
Design, Art Direction, and Production   Melissa Cabana, Back Porch Creative, Plano, TX
                                                info@BackPorchCreative.com

Cover image copyright © iStockPhoto.com.

Table of Contents

Acknowledgements

My sincere thanks to everyone who graciously listened to me talk about the ideas in this book for years before it was actually written.

A special thanks to my wife, Kathy, and children Matthew and Sarah. Their unconditional love and support makes them the best project team ever.

My thanks to these friends and authors who took the time to read through drafts and provide guidance: Adam Smith, Danise DiStasi, Laurie Beth Jones, Pam Stanton, and Tom Schenck.

And finally, a big "thank you" to the many organizations that have placed their trust in me to help their employees better manage projects. Without their continued support and feedback, this book would not have been possible.

Prologue

I originally wanted to title this book *The Project Heretic,* but I quickly learned that most people either didn't know what "heretic" means or they thought it had a negative connotation. As much as I liked the title, it didn't take a marketing genius to surmise that I needed to find a better title, so I did – but allow me to explain the "heretic" idea because I think it's relevant to why I'm writing the book.

So, what is a heretic? According to the Merriam-Webster Dictionary, a heretic is someone who believes or teaches something that goes against accepted or official beliefs.

One of the most famous heretics in history was an Italian physicist, astronomer, engineer named Galileo. You may recall that Galileo (around 1615) championed the belief that the planets revolved around the sun, not the earth. When brought in front of a Roman inquisition, he was ordered to…

> … *abstain completely from teaching or defending this doctrine and opinion or from discussing it … to abandon completely …*

the opinion that the sun stands still at the center of the world and the earth moves, and henceforth not to hold, teach, or defend it in any way whatever, either orally or in writing.
– The Inquisition's injunction against Galileo, 1616

Galileo didn't obey this order and eventually found himself under house arrest until he died in 1642. During that time, he wrote *Two New Sciences* and became known as the father of modern physics. This book would inspire many future physicists such as Albert Einstein, who went on to prove that the physical universe wasn't all that it was thought to be. Other heretics, especially those who took on religious norms, weren't so lucky; many of them were burned at the stake.

I'm fairly certain I'm not willing to go to the stake for what I'm going to share with you about project management, nor am I promoting my ideas to the level of importance of Galileo's or Einstein's. I trust you'll keep an open mind as you read the book and appreciate the tongue-in-cheek nature of the word "heretic" with regards to the ideas I'm sharing with you.

I've learned over the years that if you want to achieve excellence in the things you do, you must be willing to acknowledge mediocrity and rise above it. I've also learned that the pursuit of excellence in any endeavor is usually messy and some people don't readily sign on. We all can get stuck in a rut that, in time, can become so comfortable it prevents us from considering new ideas.

New ideas or insights on old practices usually reveal themselves in casual conversations. One such conversation occurred with my friend Pam Stanton, author of *The Project Whisperer – Understanding the Human Part of the Gantt Chart.* In

2010, Pam wrote this great book about her project management experiences. I've passed out a lot of copies of Pam's book. In 2011, Pam invited me to present at one of her hour-long webinars. I chose the topic "Project King for the Day." During the webinar, I spoke about some of the ideas I'm presenting in this book. (Thanks for the inspiration, Pam. I hope you purchase and give away a lot of my books, too.)

The other inspiration in writing this book came from the individuals and clients who, over the past 15 years, have asked for my help with managing their projects either by coming to a class or hiring me as a consultant. The ideas I've chosen to write about in this book have all been tested and honed. To them, it must have sounded odd that a consultant they were relying on to teach them project management skills or improve the performance of an existing project didn't like the word "scope," thought "critical path" was overrated, and was more interested in building a great work breakdown structure than a colorful Gantt chart. But the more these ideas proved to be rational and improved the performance of their projects, the more I was inspired to share them with others.

Pursuing Project Excellence

Introduction

This book is for all individuals who find themselves managing projects, no matter their experience level with project management processes and tools. Projects are not only a vital part of successful organization, but they're also an important aspect of successful careers. Early in my career, I learned that the ability to successfully manage a project makes you a valuable contributor to an organization. The purpose of this book is straightforward: to share ideas I have found along my own personal project management journey. I hope these ideas will help you better manage your projects.

To think that you have something to say that other people would pay to read requires two things: an ego and a proven expertise. As a human being, I can't deny the ego part, but before you get into the book, let me establish my credibility.

I've been managing projects of one type or another since the early 1980s. In 2000, I launched my own company, the Omega Leadership Group, with the mission to "teach and inspire a passion for excellence." These days, I spend most of my time in one of either two places – working with a project team on an existing project or in the classroom teaching project management. Both places have a common denominator: helping people improve their ability to manage projects. My clients are private and public companies, not-for-profit organizations, as well as some outstanding university executive education programs. The companies that I've had the honor to work with encompass major chemical, transportation, energy, utility, aircraft engine, aerospace, automobile manufacturing, paint/coatings, healthcare, and technology firms. Fifteen of my clients are Fortune 500 companies. My project consulting/training work has given me the opportunity to work with project teams around the world.

During the past 15 years, I have spent 580 days in a classroom environment teaching project management. Nearly 7,200 individuals have attended at least one of my project management classes. Needless to say, I've watched a lot of people respond to the process, language, tools, and definitions associated with managing projects. I've also helped numerous organizations implement the process, language, and tools on projects of all sizes and varieties, including hydroelectric facilities, truck and automobile manufacturing plants, aircraft engines, a 9-1-1 call center, and an open-heart surgery facility, just to name a few. It's been a great journey and I truly enjoy each day I'm helping a client with a project or in the classroom teaching project management. This isn't my job or my career. It's my calling.

The classroom is a great laboratory in which to hone the processes, language, tools, and definitions of project management. It gives you the opportunity to really explore what works and what doesn't work. I totally agree with Yogi Bhajan's adage that "if you want to learn something, read about it. If you want to understand, write about it. If you want to master something, teach it." The classroom environment exposes the instructor to questions posed by adult learners, which forces the teacher to process the information from every imaginable perspective.

Most adults who attend my classes have never before attended a formal class on project management. However, the vast majority of them are managing projects as part of their day-to-day responsibilities. Each week of the year, I have the opportunity to watch business professionals respond to the processes, language, tools, and definitions associated with project management. I have the privilege of observing the "ah-ha" and "lights-click-on" moments when they connect their on-the-job knowledge with a practical concept taught in the classroom. It's my hope that these moments prompt them to take what they've learned back to their organizations and improve their projects.

Now, hopefully, with some credibility established, let's start this journey. Here's to the pursuit of project excellence – a journey that should never end.

chapter 1

I'm Not a Fan
of the Word 'Scope'

Maybe I should ease into this heretic stuff, but what the heck. I'd rather come right out of the chute with my thoughts on the word that seems most associated with project failure: SCOPE. Anyone who has attended one of my project management classes will tell you that early in the class, someone wins my prestigious "scope" award. This award (a travel-size bottle of Scope mouthwash) is given to the individual who first mentions the word "scope" in class. As the class chuckles, I find myself explaining to the unexpected winner that it's not a personal hygiene issue – just an issue I have with the word "scope." What's interesting is that the word is usually first mentioned during an exercise where the participants identify reasons why projects fail. It doesn't take long for someone to mention "scope creep."

Earlier, I referred to project management as a language. I often start a class by explaining this will really be a language class – for some a foreign language, which most of us never really liked when we had to take them – the language associated with managing projects. One of my favorite quotes comes from Ludwig Wittgenstein, an Austrian-born philosopher who taught at Cambridge University from 1929 to 1947. "You cannot enter any world for which you do not have the language."

Project management is no different. To enter its world, you must have the language. Since projects are accomplished with teams and in organizations, I've found that projects can better be accomplished when everyone is speaking the same language. Through my work with executive education providers, I've seen first-hand the benefit of an organization sending a large group of their employees through a project management class. Afterward, they're all speaking a common language, which significantly improves project communication. (Lack of communication is a major reason identified for project failure.)

The fifth edition of the Project Management Institute's *A Guide to Project Management Body of Knowledge (PMBOK® Guide)* contains six terms associated with the word scope: product scope, product scope definition, project scope, project scope management, project scope statement and just scope. Of the hundreds of people I've asked to give me their definition of scope over the years, I've seldom heard a consistent definition. If I were teaching you a foreign language (something you wouldn't want me to do), I'm quite sure you would want me to stay away from teaching you words that have multiple meanings. This is how I feel about the word "scope." Anyone who has been around projects would agree that clear communication is a vital part of successful projects. When a group of people on the same project team all have a different understanding of what "scope" means, I would suggest the project is already off to a poor start. Some people have a very broad definition of scope, and others – such as technically oriented people – typically have a more narrow definition. So when someone mentions "scope creep," are we all really on the same page as to what is creeping?

Many people mention scope as one of the first things they have to get their arms around at the start of a project. They talk about writing out scope statements or the need to define the scope of the project. Interestingly, the fifth edition of *PMBOK®Guide* doesn't introduce the term "scope" until the Planning Process Group (after the initiation processes are completed).

Phases of a Project

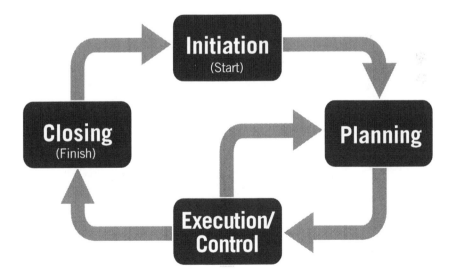

Note: I understand that the *PMBOK® Guide* refers to Initiation, Planning, Executing, Monitoring and Controlling, and Closing as Process Groups. It's my experience that this is a confusing concept, so for purposes of this book, I will refer to them as "phases."

Project Scope –
the work performed to deliver a product, service, or result with the specified features and functions.

Even though I believe and teach that you don't need to use the word "scope" to successfully manage a project (don't forget I'm a heretic), my preferred definition of scope is PMI's Project Scope definition (shown above). However, by slightly revising this definition, I think you get even more clarity: "The sum of the activities (work) performed to accomplish the project's deliverables (product, service, or result) to the agreed-upon requirements." This definition promotes a hierarchy of terms that is critical to successful projects: Activities create deliverables, deliverables are what get created to ensure the project's goal, and objectives are achieved. When you use this hierarchy, you actually don't need the word "scope." You can now communicate more clearly by telling me you have *activity* creep, *deliverable* creep, *requirement* creep and/or *business need/goal* creep. At least I'll know where your problem is, and we can begin solving it.

Project Hierarchy

1. **Business Need/Goal** – Why are we doing this project?

2. **Deliverables/Requirements** – What do we need to create to achieve the Business Need/Goal?

3. **Activities** – How are we going to create the Deliverables?

No matter what definition of "scope" you use, be sure all your team members are using the same definition, ensuring effective communication and control of the project. This will also ensure they're all on the same page as to what exactly is creeping should someone mention scope creep at the next project meeting.

PMI includes the word "scope" in their definition of the Work Breakdown Structure (WBS), a planning phase tool. *The PMBOK® Guide* (Fifth Edition) defines WBS as "a hierarchical decomposition of the total scope of work to be carried out by the project team to accomplish the project objectives and create the required deliverables." In short, the WBS is the project management tool that documents all the activities (work) necessary to create the deliverables and, therefore, achieve the business need/goal of the project.

Work Breakdown Structure

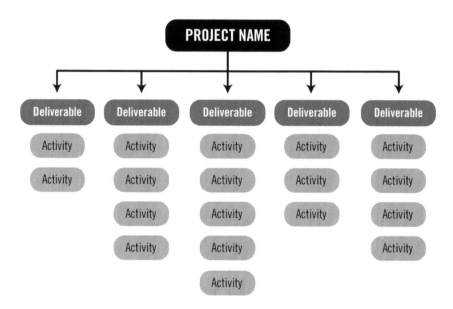

When I took the Project Management Professional (PMP®) exam in 2005, the correct answer to the question, "Which project management tool best defines the total scope of the project?" was the WBS. My experience with projects tells me that **the WBS is the single most important tool in project management.** You're going to be in a lot of trouble assigning resources, determining the costs necessary to develop a budget, specifying durations, and building a schedule if you haven't first accurately identified all the work (activities) you need to accomplish in order to complete the project. I'll talk more about issues associated with accurately identifying activities in Chapters Three and Four. And by the way, I don't like that PMI removed "deliverable-oriented" from their fifth edition definition of the WBS. "Deliverable-oriented" implies that you must understand the deliverables and their requirements first before you create the WBS. Your WBS will only be as strong as the strength of your understanding of the deliverables (product, service, or result) and their requirements.

One last thought on the work breakdown structure: As I mentioned before, I believe it's the single most important tool in project management. Two of the three triple constraints (time and cost) associated with managing a project are dependent on your knowledge of the project's activities. If you'd like more information on the value of work breakdown structures, I'd recommend reading *Work Breakdown Structures: The Foundation for Project Management Excellence,* written in 2008 by Eric Norman, Shelly Brotherton, and Robert Fried. (Note the concept of excellence.) Here's some solid advice if you want to improve your projects – identify and obsess about the project's activities, who's doing them, how long they will take, and their sequence. You'll be rewarded for this obsession in many ways as you'll learn in upcoming chapters.

An interesting side note: When picking up the classroom at the end of a class, I'll often find the bottle of Scope mouthwash sitting alone at an empty table. I still think they understood my point.

Questions to Ponder

- Does your team/company have a common definition of "scope"?

- Is everyone on the same page as to what is actually creeping should someone mention "scope creep"?

- Would your project communication be clearer if you banned the use of the word "scope" and instead used a more definitive term, such as deliverables, requirements, or activities?

chapter 2

Get Clear (and Get Signatures) on Requirements

It made sense to me to follow up the chapter on "scope" with a chapter on "requirements" since many people see the two words as synonymous. Unlike scope, the good news is that requirements can only come from one place – the project's customers. The bad news is that you first have to identify those customers and then effectively communicate with them (listen and read intently) in order to gather the requirements. This is commonly referred to as the "voice of the customer." Admittedly, this can be a very difficult part of a project. It has been my experience, and the experiences of the many project teams I've worked with, that customers don't always understand and/or communicate their requirements clearly. The "quality" of the project is only going to be measured by the response the customers have to the final products, services, or results the project delivers. I've found they're most thrilled when the final deliverables meet their requirements. I see way too many projects where the project team does not have a clear understanding of the customer's requirements and yet they're moving full speed ahead on the project.

A real-world example of this was in evidence on a recent conference call I had with a customer regarding a project that hadn't gone well. During the conversation, my client mentioned the word "simple" when discussing a particular deliverable. I asked, "What do you mean by simple?" Silence. Then I asked, "Who defined simple?" Silence. Clearly the project's customer hadn't found the deliverable they received at the end of the project simple, and as a result, they were rejecting the deliverable. This was a technology deliverable defined by a 21-year-old as surprisingly simple, but the 56-year-old's definition was much different. Watch out for words like "simple," "more efficient," "faster," and "high quality" when describing deliverables. Words like these shouldn't be used in projects without clearly defined and agreed-upon metrics.

There are a lot of words that can be substituted for "requirements": features, functions, expectations, needs, aversions, demands, conditions, etc. For the purpose of this book, I'm going to stick with requirements. I've noticed in the last few years that "requirements management" is getting a lot more attention.

Just a quick point about the term "requirements management." It's hard to manage something if you don't first know clearly what it is. The process of first identifying "requirements" is part of "requirements management," but this infers that you'll need to "manage" them throughout the project. I'll talk more about this later.

The Project Management Institute's 2014 *Pulse of the Profession®* research found that only 49 percent of organizations have the resources in place to do requirements management properly; only one-third say their leadership values requirements management as a critical competency for projects and strategic initiatives; and 53 percent fail to use a formal process to validate requirements in an unbiased way. This report also revealed that "inaccurate requirements gathering" remains a primary cause of project failure. The research noted that 5 cents of every dollar spent on a project is wasted due to poor requirements management.

To drive home the importance of clearly defining requirements in my classes, I will often show the popular YouTube video "The Expert." (If you're not one of the more than 11 million people who have seen this video, Google it.) In this short, well-acted video, a company is meeting with the client to clarify the project's requirements. The client is asking them to draw seven red lines – all of them perpendicular, some with green ink and some with transparent ink. As you can imagine, the meeting goes downhill from here, eventually ending up with the customer asking if one of the red lines can be drawn in the shape of a kitten. We all know why this is so funny, because it has happened to all of us who have ever been involved in a project. There's also a great Dilbert cartoon where Dilbert tells his project sponsor (the pointy-haired boss), "I can't start the project because the user won't give me his requirements," to which the sponsor responds, "Start making something anyway. Otherwise we'll look unhelpful."

It's been my observation, both in and out of the classroom, that there are four root causes to poor requirements management:

1. Senior management/project sponsors don't demand it;

2. Project managers don't identify within the project team who's responsible for doing it;

3. Customers don't understand and/or clearly communicate what they want; and,

4. Deliverable owners (members of the project team) don't elicit them.

So here's my advice to senior managers and project sponsors: Demand it. To project managers: Assign each of the project's deliverables to a member of the project team and give them the responsibility to gather and manage requirements. To customers (both internal and external): Do a better job of clearly communicating your requirements upfront with the project team (preferably in writing).

When I'm working with clients on either an existing project or an upcoming project, deliverables and requirements are the first areas I focus on. They go hand-in-hand. This focus establishes clarity and ownership upfront, creating a nucleus throughout the project and stability in managing project changes that will inevitably come later in the project. At some point before the project team enters the planning phase, the deliverables and their requirements need to be documented and approved. I've found the best place to do that is on the Project Charter or Statement of Work created during the initiation phase. Not only should the requirements be found in one of these documents, they should also be prioritized by the customer (in agreement with the project team member who is responsible for the particular deliverable the requirements are associated with). In addition, it's a good idea to prioritize requirements into three categories: must-haves, nice-to-haves, and highly desired. These categories will help later in the project should you run into time or cost issues (by allowing you to already know what requirements the customer is willing to give up). Projects are always a trade-off of the triple constraints: requirements, cost, and time.

Triple Constraints

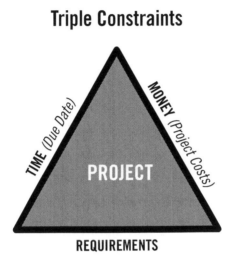

Two final thoughts when it comes to requirements:

1) Be aware of conflicting requirements. If you're asked to build a car and two of your requirements for the car are 0 to 60 miles per hour in 4 seconds and 45 miles per gallon, you can't meet them both (unless you drop the vehicle from an airplane, in which case you'll probably violate the requirement that the customer wants the car in one piece when it's delivered). If you can't see eye-to-eye with the customer about conflicting requirements, then maybe this is a project you should walk (or run) away from.

2) Many projects are initiated because there is a problem that needs to be solved. Defining the problem is not the same as defining the requirements associated with the solution(s) to the problem. Keep your conversations solution-focused. A great way to do this is to ask "Why?" a lot.

Questions to Ponder

- What can you do to improve how you identify and manage requirements?

- Are the requirements for your projects well documented and signed off?

- Are you doing a good job of controlling requirements while the project is underway?

Critical Path Is Overrated

Well, if Chapter One didn't encourage you to accept my heretic qualifications, then allow me to take on yet another pillar of project management: critical path. I've heard and read so many different definitions of critical path that it makes my head spin. In November 2013, I received an email blog about critical path from a best-selling author of some of my favorite business and marketing books. I don't know why this author felt the need to address this topic. In his blog, he defined critical path as "the longest string of dependent, non-compressible tasks." He almost got it right until he used "non-compressible." I know during my career of managing projects, I've had to compress a lot of critical path activities in order to meet aggressive finish dates. I sent him an email to question him, and he graciously responded. He concluded our brief email exchange by agreeing to disagree.

I've had the same type of dialogue with many clients and classroom participants. People involved in projects have a curiosity to learn more about critical path as evidenced by how early in the classroom (or on an actual project) they start asking what critical path is. Scope still wins that poor definition race, but critical path isn't far behind.

So what is "critical path"?

Critical Path –
the sequence of activities that represents the longest path through a project, which determines the shortest possible duration.

Though I'll get some puzzled looks when I share the *PMBOK®* *Guide* definition, this is a solid definition. The problem is that before you can fully understand and apply it, you must first understand the concepts of activities, sequences (paths), and durations. And herein lies a significant obstacle to project excellence.

After introducing the concept of critical path and having participants determine by hand (no software) where it is on the Activity Network Diagram (sometimes called Network Diagram) they've just created, I'll ask, "What five things in the project management process must be accurate in order to determine an accurate critical path(s)?" Besides the big stuff, such as a clearly defined business need/goal and well-defined deliverables/ requirements, what do you think the five things are?

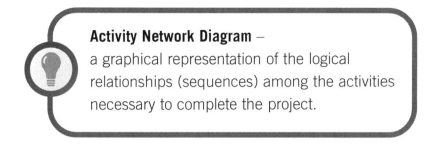

Activity Network Diagram –
a graphical representation of the logical
relationships (sequences) among the activities
necessary to complete the project.

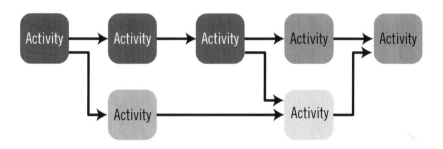

The problem of overreliance on the critical path(s) rears its head on actual projects I get involved in as well. I'll have a project team report that they've identified the critical path of the project, which is often viewed as a milestone point during the planning phase of the project. The team is very enthusiastic about showing me this accomplishment. However, when I ask to review their WBS, sequencing, resource allocation, duration estimates, and start/finish dates, I usually get blank stares or muttering about how they weren't able to get complete and accurate information on these items. Oops! I just gave you the answers to the question I asked.

If any of these are missing or inaccurate, it affects your ability to determine an accurate and, therefore, usable critical path. And frankly, other than on a project that you've had a lot of experience with, what are the odds that these five things are going to be accurate? About the same odds that a turtle can fly.

What five things must be accurate in order for the critical path to be accurate?

1. Activity list (WBS)

2. Activity dependencies (Activity Network Diagram)

3. Activity resource allocations

4. Activity duration estimates

5. Activity start/finish dates

So, why do people put so much trust in the critical path(s) of their project? Critical path(s) is not something you're owed in the project management process; it's something you earn. In class I describe the critical path as a gift the project management process gives you because you've "behaved" up to that point. Sounds a lot like the warnings we heard as children before Christmas.

I suspect one of the culprits for this fascination with critical path is project management software. PM software does not operate on the premise that the quality of what you get out is based on the quality of what you put in. The problem is that software can't assess the quality of the information entered. If you put it in, the software assumes it is right and will show you the critical path(s) at the click of a mouse. If I were to design PM software, I would make a series of pop-up windows when you click on the "show me the critical path button" that ask, "Have you accurately identified all the project's activities?" If your answer is "no," my software won't show you the critical path(s). "Have you accurately determined the sequences of all the activities?" Again, if your answer is "no," my software will not show you the critical path(s) of your project. You get the idea. My PM software would force you to behave or no critical path(s) gift for you!

A fair question is: What should you do if you can't determine an accurate critical path(s) for your project? My recommendation is that you treat each activity (except the obvious ones) as critical path (must start and finish on time in order to complete the project on time) and pray for divine intervention. Some of you may retort the odds of hoping that all the project's activities start and finish on time is right up there with my earlier reference to turtles flying.

You may have noted I'm using "path(s)" in this chapter. I've met people who believe a project can only have one critical path, but this just isn't true. A project can (and often does) have more than one critical path. An accurate critical path(s) can be a very valuable tool for making decisions in a project, decisions that involve managing risks, resources, vendors and, of course, time. Two of the biggest benefits that come from an accurate critical path(s) are:

1. The ability to identify which activities have float (can afford to be delayed and not affect the finish date), and

2. The ability to compress a project schedule to achieve an earlier-than-possible (or unrealistic) due date.

These are extremely valuable pieces of information to know if you want to effectively manage a project. Just remember – you have to earn the gift!

Questions to Ponder

- How credible are the critical path(s) you're using in your projects?

- Besides the direct items mentioned, what other items influence the ability to determine an accurate critical path(s)?

- After laying out the Activity Network Diagram and determining the critical path(s), what should be your next step?

chapter 4

Never Build a
Schedule Backward

You should see the looks I get when I suggest that you should not build a project schedule backward from a proposed finish date. This definitely is a common practice in a lot of organizations. (Note I didn't use the words "best practice.") Before I start down this path, let me say that for projects you've successfully completed (meaning with schedules that have proven to work), I don't have any problem with the schedule being built backward from the finish date.

From my experience with many projects across many different organizations, I've learned you can count on one thing: The due date imposed at the beginning of the project will most likely be unrealistic when compared to the actual amount of work that must be done. Why? Because the date was determined not by the actual amount of work to complete the project, but rather by a date committed to by senior management or marketing/sales. The sooner you accept this reality, the sooner this chapter will make sense to you.

I've tested this approach in hundreds of classes and across hundreds of actual projects. Even though the initial reaction is, "That's not how our company does projects," people usually agree by the end of our time together that they've learned a better way. I can't change the reality of unrealistic due dates placed on projects, but I can recommend a better way to deal with them than building the schedule backward.

A strong point for not building schedules backward from an arbitrarily chosen due date is that it legitimizes the due date! And, once you've done that, you'll have a whole lot of stakeholders thinking you're going to get the project done on time. (I wish I could end the chapter here, but I don't want to leave you hanging.)

Instead of building the schedule backward, I've found it's better practice to identify the activities (create the WBS), then sequence the activities logically, left to right (build the Activity Network Diagram), then add resources and durations without establishing any start/finish dates yet for the activities.

Next, determine the critical path(s) and ask yourself how comfortable you are with their accuracy (see Chapter Three). Then, select a doable project start date (based on the availability of your resources), then put start/finish dates on each activity, from left to right.

If you discover the finish date is beyond the original proposed date, you now know you'll need to work with the project team to compress the schedule. You'll also know you're working on a time-driven project. A time-driven project is one in which you'd be willing to spend more money and/or reduce the requirements (quality) in order to meet an aggressive or unrealistic due date. I find that clients are often uneasy with the term "unrealistic" when discussing a project's due date. One of the participants in a class defined "time-driven" in a more politically correct manner: when the time constraints of the project are believed to be unmanageable under normal circumstances. Though I like this definition, it's not the role of a heretic to be politically correct.

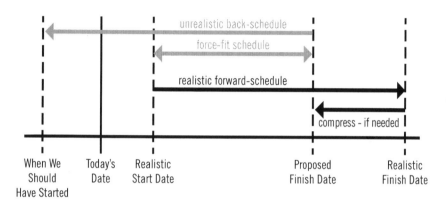

Once you've determined that the finish date of your left-to-right schedule goes beyond the proposed due date, this information needs to be communicated to key stakeholders, especially the project's sponsor. Who knows, once they're presented with the realistic finish date, maybe they'll move the due date to match your schedule. Don't hold your breath for this miracle to happen. Instead, get the project team together and start working to identify ways to compress the schedule. Here's where the work you did to accurately identify activities, sequences, and durations pays off. You'll be confident using the critical path(s) to make the tough decisions.

Between my work in the classroom and on real-world projects, I've identified 12 specific techniques (see end of chapter for details) for compressing activities on a schedule. Surprisingly, only one involves throwing more resources at the project. In the event you try every compression technique known to man and still can't meet the proposed due date, it's time for a serious meeting with your project's sponsor and customers.

There's one other problem with developing schedules right-to-left and that's with the development of the duration of the project's activities. Duration estimates for the activities should always come from the person or entity doing the activity. Why? Because they should know best the effort necessary to complete the activity and the calendar time (duration) associated with the effort after they factor in their other project and operational commitments. Of course, it's the duration you use to build the schedule. This information should always come from the "bottom up," not from the "top down." Herein lies the other problem with right-to-left scheduling. Most durations are dictated to the person doing the activity from the "top down" instead of being owned by the resource from the "bottom up." Buy-in from the people actually doing the work (activities) associated with the project is a big factor of successful projects.

In conclusion, I'm recommending that instead of building a right-to-left schedule and legitimizing an unrealistic proposed due date, you should build the schedule from left to right. Then, if the finish date is beyond the initially proposed due date, either plead for mercy, pray for a miracle, or compress the right-to-left schedule. I believe you'll find that, when you work to compress the schedule, you'll be making better decisions. I know what you're thinking: pure heresy.

It is not heresy. It is a proven best practice that, when implemented, results in delivering the agreed-upon deliverables on time.

The process involves 12 techniques for compressing project activities:

1. Focus on compressing activities occurring earlier in the schedule rather than later. (Don't put all your compression eggs in the end-of-the-project basket.)

2. Consider outsourcing any critical path activities if it will reduce their durations or the risk associated with them. (Often expensive, but it works.)

3. Add additional resources to reduce durations. (I can't advise you as to where to find these additional resources; people are most likely already avoiding you if you're a project manager.)

4. Work overtime and weekends. (This will make you a hero with the project team.)

5. Redefine hours in a working day or go to shifts to better utilize the 24 hours in a day.

6. If you have offices around the country or world, shift work to different time zones. (It's always happy hour somewhere!)

7. Start the project sooner. (Duh!)

8. Assess if any critical path activities could be moved into parallel (done at the same time) without adding too much additional risk.

9. Decompose critical path activities into sub-activities. This may allow you to find sub-activities that can be done in parallel and/or develop more accurate durations – both of which may allow you to reduce the activity's initial duration.

10. Redefine deliverable requirements with the customer in an effort to reduce activities. (This will require a revised project charter and work breakdown structure.)

11. Negotiate with the customer to see if the project deliverables could be delivered in phases based on the customer's needs.

12. Instead of adding more resources, negotiate with the project sponsor to get a higher level of commitment from the resources that are already assigned to the project. (This is my favorite and, in my opinion, a much better technique than #3.)

Questions to Ponder

- Are too many of your projects time-driven? Why?

- What are some techniques you've used to successfully compress a schedule?

- How does your organization develop durations for the project's activities?

chapter 5

Gantt Charts Can Be Optional

Since the early 1900s, when Henry Gantt developed the Gantt chart, it has been the primary tool that project managers have used to develop and communicate the project timeline/ schedule. Maybe it's time we give its value a second look.

I like Gantt charts and believe they offer some unique visuals you can't find with other scheduling tools. But over the past few years, I've become a proponent of the Activity Network Diagram. Why? Because I've watched project teams (in and out of the classroom) create them, and it's a more collaborative and engaging process. Usually, a Gantt chart is created by a single project team member sitting in front of a computer screen. Many individuals are more comfortable with creating an Activity Network Diagram because it's similar to flow charting, value stream mapping, and process mapping – 21st-century tools that have become more commonplace in organizations today as a result of quality and process-improvement efforts.

Even if the project team is going to use a Gantt chart, I still recommend developing an Activity Network Diagram first. I've not met a student or client yet who has had difficulty creating it, understanding it, or seeing the value in doing it first. I agree that the Activity Network Diagram doesn't have some of the visuals – bars whose lengths represent durations and a calendar across the top – you'll find on a Gantt chart, but when you can create it with sticky notes in a room full of engaged project team members, you'll have greater ownership. I'll trade off fancy visuals for engagement and ownership any day. Of course, if you decide you want a Gantt chart, you can transfer your sticky-note Activity Network Diagram into PM software, find a big printer, and print out the end product. Or, be bold and put start/finish dates on your sticky notes and run the project from the Activity Network Diagram. I actually use this technique when I'm working with clients who are not interested in investing in PM software and large printers.

A few years ago, I had the opportunity to work with a project team that was putting together an open-heart surgery facility. The project entailed renovating two existing operating rooms to handle heart surgeries and putting together a small cardio-vascular intensive care unit. The team was great, but they had little experience with project management. Instead of developing an intimidating (and expensive) Gantt chart, we ran the project off an Activity Network Diagram created with sticky notes attached to a length of butcher paper hung on a conference room wall. I wish I had taken a picture of that diagram with the project team in front of it. As we completed activities, we simply put a red "X" across the sticky note. Consider another benefit of an Activity Network Diagram created with sticky notes: If there's a power failure or your computers go down, at least you'll still be able to manage your project!

I suppose you can't write a book about project management without mentioning PM software. I've found PM software can encourage some bad habits when managing projects. As of the writing of this book, I've begun using an open-source (that means "free") software called ProjectLibre, which appears to have all the bells and whistles that a project team needs to plan, track, and control a project. I'm also a big fan of WBS Schedule Pro, a software product developed by Critical Tools in Austin, Texas. This software allows you to create an activity list, transfer it into a WBS format, and create an Activity Network Diagram (Critical Tools uses Network Diagram), complete with resources, durations, start/finish dates, and critical path(s). During the writing of this book, Critical Tools updated this software to include the ability to create a Gantt chart as well. I'd strongly recommend checking out both of these products. But please do me a favor: Don't use software designed for creating spreadsheets! Project schedules need to be created using software that allows the schedule to show dependencies and can be easily updated while the project is ongoing.

Questions to Ponder

• Is the time and effort to create a Gantt chart really adding value to your projects?

• Is the team involved in creating the Gantt chart, or does someone just go off and create it in the solitude of their cubicle?

• Can you see the value in having the project team engaged in creating the sequence of activities with sticky notes before creating a Gantt chart?

chapter 6

Fumbles Are Discouraged

All projects have one thing in common: at least one customer waiting patiently (or impatiently) at the end of the project to receive a deliverable (product, service, or result) that meets their requirements (see Chapter Two). It should be the desire of every project sponsor, manager, and team to ensure that the project's customers are satisfied (delighted is even better) with the deliverables handed off to them. This is a crucial handoff – one that can't afford to be fumbled. At this moment, the ultimate success of the project is measured.

As I've already stated, the preparation for this handoff actually starts upfront by clearly identifying and agreeing on the customer's requirements. So how do we know if the customer likes the deliverables at the end of the project? What if they won't really know if they like the deliverables until they've had an opportunity to use them over a period of time?

Since we're on the topic of fumbles, I thought you might like to know that during the 2014 National Football League (NFL) season there were 674 fumbles. Of these, 308 were recovered by the team that fumbled. No surprise here, but quarterbacks lead the NFL in fumbles because they handle the ball more than any other player during a game. Clearly, fumbles are a part of the game of football. They're also a part of projects. But just like in football, you should do everything you can to minimize them. And here's how:

In Chapter Two, I addressed ways to avoid fumbles upfront by adequately defining requirements. There is another upfront technique not often considered by project teams. This approach aligns with what a project team should do at the end of a project to ensure their customers are satisfied with the final deliverables. I call this technique "identifying transitional deliverables."

Transitional Deliverable –
a product, service, or mechanism that bridges the gap between when a customer receives a deliverable and when the customer can determine if the deliverable meets their requirements.

This gap can be huge on some projects. For example, let's say I launch a project to reduce defects by 10 percent in a product we're currently manufacturing. At the end of the project, I hand you (my customer) some new tools and a new process that will surely reduce defects by 10 percent (or at least it did during the testing we did during the project). I drop these new tools and new process off on your desk and say, "Good luck." Clearly my project's done and now yours is just beginning.

This is an example of a poor handoff and will most likely result in a project "fumble."

Instead, we should have identified upfront in the Initiation Phase a "transitional" deliverable, which establishes a method for tracking and measuring the implementation of the new tools and process to verify defects were being reduced during production. This changes the end of the project from "Here are the new tools and process. Good luck." to "This project isn't completed until we have the data confirming defects have been consistently reduced by 10 percent."

Another example of a transitional deliverable includes when one of the project's main deliverables is a new product or service. Can a customer really evaluate the quality of a new product or service before they've had an opportunity to use it over a period of time? Software projects are a good example of this. Most customers usually need to use the software for a while before they can evaluate its effectiveness. If you survey them a couple of weeks after you supply the software, they might even find a couple of features they didn't initially think of. This gives you the opportunity to quote a follow-up project for version 2.0.

For software projects, creating a help desk or training users are examples of transitional deliverables. I usually like to put transitional deliverables into a final phase of the project called the "handoff" or "transition phase." This helps get the team thinking upfront that transitional deliverables may need to be identified. The work in this final phase focuses on making sure there are no fumbles between the completion of the project and the operational side of the organization or the external customer. This is especially beneficial for strategic projects or projects that involve implementing a procedural change. Fumbles during the handoff of these projects can have dire consequences.

Another important aspect of the handoff/transition phase is that the entire project team doesn't always need to be involved. If this is the case, formally close out the main portion (phases) of the project and release those team members who were responsible for deliverables that didn't require transition. These team members can move on to other projects (or get reacquainted with their loved ones). A smaller team will then remain to handle the transitional work.

I appreciate that there are times when we can't wait to say goodbye (or good riddance) to a customer at the end of the project; just don't say goodbye too soon. Deliverables handed over to the customer at the end of a project should never be treated like hot potatoes or live hand grenades. You could be missing the opportunity for follow-up business with an external customer or the opportunity to build a stronger relationship with an internal customer. Whatever you do, make sure the handoff at the end of the project is smooth, which guarantees a satisfied customer.

Questions to Ponder

- Are you using transitional deliverables in your projects?

- Are you following up after your projects to see if the customer(s) is satisfied with what you delivered to them?

- Could your organization be missing out on follow-up business because of the lack of follow-through on projects?

Final Thoughts

My life's mission is to teach and inspire a passion for excellence. Throughout history, it's often been the role of the heretic to challenge the status quo and point out a better way.

I trust that some, if not all, of the ideas I covered in this book inspire you to continue learning, challenging, and improving the process and tools you use to manage projects. My goal wasn't to make my point and then walk away, but rather to create a catalyst to improve the processes in which organizations and employees depend on daily to successfully accomplish projects. Agree or disagree, if I prompted you to say, "This is the way we've always done it," and then you question whether that way is actually working or in your best interests, then I've been successful.

Sources

A Guide to the Project Management Body of Knowledge (PMBOK® Guide) (Fifth Edition). Project Management Institute. 2013.

The High Cost of Low Performance, PMI's Pulse of the Profession, Project Management Institute. 2014.

Dilbert, by Scott Adams.

Work Breakdown Structures: The Foundation for Project Management, by Eric Norman, Shelly Brotherton and Robert Fried.

Yogi Bhajan® quote – Kundalini Research Institute.

The Project Whisperer, by Pam Stanton.

"Understanding Critical Path," Nov. 15, 2013, blog by Seth Godin.

About the Author

Bob Jewell is the Founder/Chief Excellence Officer of the Omega Leadership Group, LLC in West Chester, Ohio.

Besides his work with corporate and nonprofit clients, Bob is associated with the executive education programs at Kent State University, Miami University, and the University of Dayton.

Bob earned a bachelor's degree in welding engineering from The Ohio State University in 1980 and received his Project Management Professional (PMP®) certification from the Project Management Institute in 2005.

Made in the USA
Monee, IL
30 September 2020